WAV⟋ ⟍

celtic pi⟍   ⟋ourney

Meditations and Prayers
from Aotearoa New Zealand

WAYMARKS

for the
Celtic Pilgrim Journey

Meditations and Prayers
from Aotearoa New Zealand

CRAIG A. ROBERTS

ANAMCHARA
BOOKS

© Craig A. Roberts 2024

Vestal, New York 13850
www.AnamcharaBooks.com

paperback ISBN: 978-1-62524-912-8
eBook ISBN: 978-1-62524-913-5

Scripture Quotations:

SAAS: Old Testament text quoted from St Athanasius Academy
Septuagint TM. Copyright © 2008 by St Athanasius Academy of
Orthodox Theology. Used by permission. All rights reserved.

EOB: New Testament text quoted from Eastern/Greek Orthodox
New Testament.© Laurent Cleenewerck, Editor, 2007–2015, revised
for this edition in 2015. Used by permission. All rights reserved.

to Dave & Anita

Pilgrims' Journey

We are partakers of God
through the Holy Spirit.

We are transformed by God
through the power of the Cross.

We become made fully human,
the image of Christ—the glory of God.

It's an intimate journey
with our Triune God.

CONTENTS

Notes on Poetic Language

You will come across some Scots Gaelic (the indigenous language of the Scottish Highlands) and Maori (the indigenous language of Aotearoa New Zealand) phrases in this book. I use them intentionally to deepen the moment of imagery and reflection. When our eyes encounter an unfamiliar word, we automatically pause a moment, creating a moment for the Holy Trinity to enter more fully into our reading. Words of Indigenous people also take our imagery back in time, allowing us to glimpse our world from another perspective.

A short glossary follows next with the meanings of these words.

Glossary

Scots Gaelic Phrases

An Gèadh Fiadhaich: "The Wild Goose," a poetic name for the Holy Spirit, untamed by humanity.

Anam-charaid (*Anamchara* in Irish): Soul friend.

Deòir Dhè: Tears of God.

Dhè: The one God who is *Cruithear* (Creator), *Ìosa Crìost* (Jesus Christ), and *An Gèadh Fiadhaich* (Holy Spirit), all in relationship. We are partakers of God through the Holy Ghost; we are transformed by God through the power of the Cross; we become fully human in the image of Christ, which is the glory of God.

Dùthchas nan Gàidheal: The focal web of belief and kinship of Gaelic people.

Ìosa Crìost: The name of Jesus Christ I enjoy using. The English name has become overly used and misused, but when we encounter an unfamiliar word for the Son of God, we automatically stop, think, and wonder, "Who is this?" This allows us to commune afresh with Christ's Divinity.

Solas Chrìost: Christ's Light

Sorchar nan Ruel: "Lightener of the Stars," the Scots' poetic name for Jesus Christ.

Sùil an Latha: "Eye of the Day," the Scots' poetic name for the sun.

Trasna: Trasna is the place of crossing over (for example, crossing over a stormy mountain range through a dangerous pass).

Maori Phrases

Kuaka: Bar-tailed godwit. This bird journeys from Arctic to Antipodes in one single flight.

Korimako: Bellbird. A forest bird with the purest sound made in birdsong.

Kōtuku-ngutupapa: Royal spoonbill. These birds migrated from Australia, flying over the Tasman Sea to settle in Aotearoa New Zealand.

Kowhai: A winter flowering tree covered in yellow blooms that is a rich source of nectar.

Paua: Large molluscs whose shells have reflective spectrum of colours. They are one of the most colorful shells in the world.

Pīpīwharauroa: Shining cuckoo. This is a migratory bird that breeds in Aotearoa New Zealand.

Riroriro: Grey warbler. This forest bird is more often heard than seen. It is one of the smallest of birds in Aotearoa New Zealand.

Tangata whenua: Maori, the people who are indigenous to the land Aotearoa New Zealand.

Tangata Tiriti: People of the Treaty. All immigrant people and their descendants settle and reside under the terms of Aotearoa New Zealand's founding treaty. The Treaty of Waitangi is between the British Crown and Maori.

Toroa: Antipodean albatross. This is a wonderful bird that cruises over the Southern Ocean; longline fishing is the greatest threat to its survival.

Foreword

This poetic treasury touches the deep springs of emotion. As a result, it will long reside in our memories and sustain us in dark times. The author is a fighter, an athlete of the Spirit. Nothing he writes here is confection. It reveals vulnerability. It brings prophetic challenge. Above all it wings us into the Presence.

The Eastern Church cultivates *phronema*—the mind of Christ that plumbs the depth of the soul, the width of the universe, and the essence of Jesus' Way. In the West, Celtic Christianity nurtures a similar spirituality that makes room for poetry—"the eye of the eagle" and the "five-stringed harp"—the use of sight, sound, hearing, touch, and scent in our lives on Earth with God.

This book is rooted in the Bible and in Jesus Christ, but its words are never secondhand. This book is also rooted in the birds, in Nature, and in the world of the Spirit. It will inspire you to explore untrodden places in your life.

— *Ray Simpson*, founding guardian of the international new monastic community of Aidan and Hilda; www. raysimpson.org

Author's
Preface

*C*rois *Chill Daltain* (Kildalton Cross) stands on the Isle of Mull, Scotland. Its name comes from the poetic Gaelic name for the beloved disciple, Saint John. Said to be built by monks from Iona in the style of the Pict stonemasons, it is a remarkable cross. Each face tells tales of the resurrection power of the cross; the front face of this monolithic high cross uses Pictish Pagan imagery pointing to an afterlife—symbolized by the snake—with *Ìosa Crìost* (Jesus Christ), while the opposite face is rich in biblical imagery.

This cross respectfully stands on a border between two worlds—and this book is my attempt to do the same in book form. My writing embraces the language of Creation's rhythms as I journey to be transformed into the image of *Ìosa Crìost*. Kidalton Cross speaks to me in Aotearoa New

Zealand as I interact with friends wrestling with Christianity while they embrace and explore more fully their Indigenous culture. I experience a similar dynamic as I explore the indigenous ways my Scots Gaelic forbears expressed their Christian faith from ancient to recent times.

Against the flow of our generation's ways, the grace of the Holy Trinity speaks into our condition and calls us to journey amid an Anthropocentric Age (an era centered on human beings). Our Western world has lost its way to the Tree of Life: lost is the breath of communion with our Triune God; lost is our awareness of our connection with Creation; lost is restorative grace between people; and lost is our understanding of our own innermost thoughts, the ones that drive our behaviors. Yet amid this torn veil of human understanding, the promises of God remain. Divine love and pathos for humanity and Creation soar on the wings of the wind.

Anthropologist Brian Fagan in his book *The Little Ice Age* describes how eighth-century Irish monks, skilled seamen, often followed the spring migration of wild geese as far north as Iceland. As the monks journeyed across dangerous seas toward hidden lands, they gave their trust and lives to these wild geese. The monks did not settle permanently on any isles they encountered, for these were pilgrim voyages, but as they journeyed, the monks listened for and followed the call of the Holy Spirit with a deep sensitivity and commitment, just as they followed the wild geese. Today, the name *An Gèadh Fiadhaich* ("Wild Goose") permits us to engage with the Holy Spirit with deeper Celtic intimacy. For the same reason, I use other Scots Gaelic phrases throughout my work, hoping to free us from the cages created by our contemporary world's limited imagination.

Poetic writings are how I express myself to myself—and I share them with others that they may uplift and encourage them as they too journey. This book invites the reader to voyage with *Ìosa Crìost*. It is a poetic exploration of the Holy Trinity moving amid the "otherness of life" around us. This pilgrim's voyage has no neat traceable pattern, no reliance on predicted coordinates of knowledge. Rather, this is a journey led by the Holy Spirit to reorient our Anthropocentric Age to the Tree of Life.

The wind blows where it wants to,
and you hear its sound,
but do not know where it comes
from and where it is going.
So it is with everyone born of the Spirit.

John 3:8 (EOB)

Editor's
Introduction

Historian John Hope Franklin wrote, "We must go beyond textbooks, go out into the bypaths and untrodden depths of the wilderness and travel and explore and tell the world the glories of our journey." Franklin may have been speaking of physical travel, venturing into new geographical locations—but as the ancient Celts knew, the most glorious journey is the one that leads us into the unexplored regions of our spiritual lives. This journey can lead us through forests and along seacoasts, through pastureland and city streets; it is lit by the beaming sun, the silvery cycle of the moon's phases, and the spangle of starshine. The same journey also leads us deeper into our own hearts, into the hidden recesses of our conscious-ness—and the journey leads as well into encounters with other beings, where we are challenged to release our ego's demands even as we see Divinity looking back at us from another's eyes.

For that is the goal of this journey—to deepen our awareness of God's Presence in Creation, within ourselves, and in our relationships and communities. This book offers a variety of patterns of reading and contemplation to explore the untrodden places in our lives.

How to
Use This Book

The readings in this book include poems, prayers, scripture, and stories. They are not intended to instruct or exhort; they are envisioned as catalysts that trigger unique and individual spiritual reactions in each reader. At the same time, they are meant to be signposts to guide readers on their journeys. When we venture into those "untrodden places," it's good to have some guidance.

These journeys are slow; they're meant to be. You can't read through this book quickly and hope to get anything from it. Instead, make this book part of your daily prayer time over weeks or even months. Allow each reading to serve as a jump-pad for prayer, contemplation, and journaling. You may want to spend an hour a day with each section's readings—or you might want to spend a week using the same section each morning. Move on only when you feel ready. Allow the Spirit to guide your use of this book.

Each section can also be spoken as a contemplative liturgy, ministering to the condition of a gathered people. In that case, first prayerfully discern which section will bring the Spirit to a gathering of seekers and pilgrims. Then let your voice flow through each reading, leaving space for those present to move from listening to praying. When poems, prayer, fables, and tales are told in gatherings, the Spirit can stir curious wanderers to begin their Celtic odyssey with Ìosa Crìost.

Solas Chrìost

The book begins with a short meditation on the Light of Christ. As the sixth-century Celtic saint Columbanus said, the Light of Christ kindles our individual lights so that they "receive perpetual light from the Light perpetual." He went on to say:

Do thou enrich my lantern with the light,
I pray thee, Jesus mine, so that by its light
there may be disclosed to me
those holy places of the holy,
which hold you, the eternal priest of the eternal things.

The Gospel of John has left a deep imprint on the author's poetic imagination, and he, like the Gospel author, speaks often of Christ as the Light. Craig also uses the poetic Gaelic name for Jesus Christ—*Sorchar nan Ruel*, meaning, "Lightener of the Stars." This poetic imagery points to the Person who creates Light in our lives, while it also acknowledges and honors the ancient heritage of the Gaels and Picts. These were words spoken and heard by Craig's ancestors not too many generations ago, and his modern-day use of this language invites us to embrace new ways to experience and express Christ, while at the same time, freeing ourselves of the imperial church's unhelpful cultural baggage.

Waymarks

The author has created eight waymarks for this book. Each has its own voice to guide and uplift spiritual pilgrims, but each uses the same eight tools:

- *Letter to Anam-charaid:* This is a message addressed directly to you, the reader, from the author, your soul friend, a spiritual companion on your journey.

- *The Call:* This is the focal point for each waymark.

- *Lectio Divina:* This ancient contemplative way of reading scripture (it means, literally, "divine reading") includes these four steps:

  - *Read:* Slowly read the scripture passage. Then read it again. Notice any words or images that jump out at you.

  - *Reflect:* Allow those words or images to expand in your mind.

  - *Respond:* This is your chance to respond to God in prayer or in a journal.

  - *Rest:* Sit silently for a few moments. If words and thoughts enter your mind, gently release them.

The tools that follow can be applied to the last three steps.

- *Reflection:* Allow the words to cast a "reflection" in your mind. Don't analyze or intellectualize; simply open your mind to whatever God may bring to you. Don't try to force it. Listen to whatever God may bring to mind.

- *Prayer:* Allow the words of this reading to guide you into deeper communication with God.

- *Contemplative Cue:* Contemplation is the "rest" part of lectio divina, and this "cue" is intended to serve as a focal point for a time of mental and physical stillness.

- *The Challenge of Trasna:* Trasna is the place of crossing over (for example, crossing over a stormy mountain range through a dangerous pass). *The Challenge of Trasna* means that once we choose to cross over, there is no turning back. This meditation will direct your attention to ways God may be calling you to face up to the inner and outer challenges of life.

- *Journal Entry:* This piece is the author's "journal entry," which you can use as prompt for your own journaling. Record anything you want to remember from your quiet time.

Ruminations on Praxis

"Praxis" refers to the active expression of our faith. It is the *practice* that brings our spirituality down to earth, so that it is something we *do* rather than something we think or feel. In this section, the author shows us how to integrate the practical and spiritual into a seamless whole.

Sùil an Latha

The writings in this section nudge pilgrims toward a daily rhythm of contemplation and prayer in the presence of *An Geadh Fiadhaich* (the Holy Spirit). The ancient Celts knew that everything about Nature is sacramental, expressions of Divinity—including the cycles of sun and moon, light and darkness. The readings in this section can be used to bless each stage of the day. They will help you find the Presence of the Spirit in the hours of your ordinary life.

Some Terms Defined

The author uses several words that may or may not be familiar to readers. These words include *kairos, phronema,* and *pathos.*

Kairos

Kairos is a Greek word for time—but not clock time. *Chronos* is the ancient word for time as a measurable quality, something that can be divided into sequential units such as minutes and hours. *Kairos,* on the other hand, refers to a concept outside chronology: the appointed time, God's time, the *right* time. The word originally came from both archery and weaving: the moment in which an arrow may be shot to penetrate a target is kairos, and so is the moment in which the threads on a loom are ready for the shuttle to pass through them.

We might also think of kairos as an opening in chronological time through which God's Spirit enters and acts. Like a gap in the clouds that allows the sun to cast its rays on a cloudy day, kairos is the experience of eternity in the midst of our ordinary minutes, hours, days, months, and years. It is a timeless space within time, a suspended moment that is pregnant with potential.

Phronema

Phronema is another Greek word, one that Orthodox Christianity has given a spiritual significance. The root word is *frono* (meaning "I believe"), and *phronema*'s literal meaning is "mindset" or "outlook." As a spiritual term, however, *phronema* is far more than an intellectual perspective. It is not an ideology—a way of *thinking about life*—but rather a *way of life.*

When we make the "phronema of Christ" our own, we are doing what scripture refers to as "taking on the mind of Christ" (see, for example, 1 Corinthians 2:16). This means we think and act as Christ would; we are intimately and unshakeably connected with God (as Jesus was), as well as with other human beings and the whole of Creation (as Jesus also was).

Ideologies and doctrines do not necessarily change either our inner or outer lives. We might be intellectually obsessed with studying scripture—and yet still be far from the self-giving mind of Christ. Ideas and information live only in our brains, and our egos make take pride in our intellectual belief that we have gotten everything *right*. Meanwhile, when we share Christ's phronema, we are transformed from the inside out. We surrender our egos, our pride, and even our ideas, so that we can participate with our entire beings in the love of God.

The Pathos of God

Throughout this book, the author refers to "the pathos of God." His use of this term is based on Jewish theologian Abraham J. Heschel's definition of Divine pathos in his book *The Prophets,* where he speaks of God's "passionate summons" to the world, a "dynamic relation between God and [humanity]" that Heschel names *pathos.* This relationship is not intellectual; it does not arise from doctrine or analysis but from our emotions and from God's. As we enter into relationship with God, we share Divine pathos—the pain and passion God feels for our world. Emotional experience becomes the "focal point" for our understanding of God, and we live not only our own personal lives "but also the life of God" in an intimate "living together."

According to Heschel's definition, Divine pathos is an active involvement in every aspect of our world. "The predicament of [humanity]," he writes, "is a predicament of God Who has a stake in the human situation." God chooses to make human experience and history "a consort, a partner, a factor in the life of God."

This, says Heschel, is the real state of our world: not alienation from God because of human sin but rather an active and ongoing communion. This communion is not without challenges and pain, and yet it calls out to us even amid our world's brokenness, injustice, and sorrow. Divine pathos makes possible a "living encounter" between the human heart and God.

Orthodox theologian John Behr, in his book *John the Theologian and His Paschal Gospel,* also writes about *pathos.* Behr defines pathos as the suffering we feel from the pain experienced by another being. This concept does not glorify pain but rather allows it to touch us deeply; through the Holy Spirit, we experience Christ's pain, the pathos of God. We do not then wallow in the pain, though. Instead, *pathos* demands an active response powered by the love and wisdom of the Spirit. This too is part of the pilgrim's journey, as we overcome our fears and learn to love others as Christ loves us (sharing in Christ's phronema).

May Craig Roberts' poetry and prayers guide you deeper into a living encounter with the Divine pathos that reaches out to heal our world. May you experience kairos moments as you read his words, and may you enter more fully into the phronema of Christ.

> —*Ellyn Sanna*
> Anamchara Editor

Solas Chrìost

(Christ's Light)

Glory to the One who holds the keys
to Anthropocene's redemption,
Crìost, the firstborn of all Creation,
the light of humankind, in Him is life.

He who was, who is, and is to come,
who is in the midst of God's Throne,
broods over a plague of unleashed hubris,
Creation undone by human desire.

Creation's breath wanes.
Barren souls batter Eden's gates,
defy our Creator's throne and grace;
chimeric dreams and callous hands
cultivate welter and waste.

An Gèadh Fiadhaich flies over the Earth,
a rainbow arched over Her head. She calls:
"Saints travail. Speak, Solas Chrìost.
Let your incense rise to Heaven's throne."

Out of every tribe, language, people, and nation,
pilgrims travail with An Gèadh Fiadhaich,
voyage to restore Heaven's way on Earth
with patient endurance and faith of saints.

PART I

Waymarks
for Pilgrims
Who Voyage

Waymark 1

Voyage

Letter to
Anam-charaid

Dear Anam-charaid,
your innerscape,
an interior world, a wilderness
awaiting an exodus
of tongue, heart, and deed
into alternate ways
of Heaven on Earth—
not forged by counterpressures
of secular minds.
No. A voyage formed
by the phronema
of Crìost.

The Call

Called to follow, down unknown paths,
traveling with Christ, so not alone.

Voyage beyond the horizons
of my mind into chasms of heart and soul.

Amid trial and tempest, Christ leads,
and resurrects the marrow of dry bones.

Lectio Divina

By faith, Abraham,
when he was called,
obeyed and left the place
which he was supposed to receive as his inheritance.
He left, not knowing where he was going.

—Hebrews 11:8 (EOB)

Reflection

To journey
is first to meet with Christ,
who at the strangest moment,
unlocks a padlocked door,
one I had foreclosed to a wayless place.
There He and I stand upon a threshold;
I wait till He calls me to cross.
As my bare foot touches
unknown ground,
the Holy Spirit guides my step,
but She doesn't tell me our destination.

In these borderlands,
monsters wait to wound my heart.
I wrestle against wayward tensions,
mind against soul;
my mouth utters distress.
Yet Christ removes all fear;
unites heart, mind, and soul.
I, saved from affliction,
brought into Christ's light,
breathe the Paraclete's air,
pass over another threshold,
and journey on from there.

Contemplative Cue

Let the Holy Spirit
be your Companion
across unimagined wastelands,
between mind and soul,
where lost spiritual sensibilities
become awakened
by Divine revelation.

Prayer

Deep Sojourn

It's morning.
The Holy Spirit reminds me to slow down,
move in Her gracious peace, trust Her pace.
Yet my heart plagues my mind—
imagined terrors of this unknown journey.
It bangs on the doors to my mind,
interrupts the prayers of my soul.
It's a bailiff, unrelenting at my door.
Each heartbeat bangs, "Stop!
Turn around, why go on?"

I pray in silence; my tongue's utterance
seeks to silence the noise,
rest in God's presence.
I ask:
"Let this journey unfold
in my Creator's kairos."
"Fear not," I hear.
"You are not alone. Go on."

This treasured moment
is time with Christ—solitude,
to commune in inner silence—
just Him and me,
letting Him take me deeper in.

He says: "Stop wandering around.
Come, pilgrim, sojourn with me.
I am your light, follow Me.
Journey deeper in, to hidden places
you've never known before."

I ask:
"How deep shall we go?"

"Come, pilgrim," He replies.
"Sojourn deeper,
like a goose-beaked whale
in dark depths where daylight is hidden.
Explore unseen layers of treasured virtues—
and then see how they become monsters,
devoid of My light."

"Take me there, Christ Jesus,
that I may honour You above all.
Take me there to see what is hidden,
beliefs I value yet encumber me there.
Be a light to my senses to see the unseen.
Christ, shine Your light into my deepest chasm."

The Challenge of Trasna

Soul Song
(a fable)

Deep unto deep calls out.
Desire to journey floods Kuaka's soul,
words unthought but known.

One song sung of leaving, arriving,
life wedged between two halves:
autumn farewells, spring arrivals.

Air surges: upwelling, lifting, flight.
Creator's rhythm spurs wind on wing.
Feathers light, strong, flex together.

Nine days and nights coalesce—
one day everlasting.
A fast body shrinking,
consumed in flight.

Air, pressure, tone, cadence: Kuaka.
Kuaka moves with Creator;
kith and kin sing to each other.

A-wik! a-wik!
Kuaka calls over ancient seas,
wordless songs, rich in meaning.
A void closes between soul and wing.

As Arctic's polar star dips from sight,
Antipodes Southern Cross climbs high;
soul song hymns with earth, sea, sky.

Spirit guides Kuaka's being,
subtle movements of communion.
Kuaka follows Christ's leading.

Of three treasures does Kuaka sing:
praises to God of unknown journeys,
trust in the sacred call,
and joy in the Divine Being.

Journal Entry

How does a pilgrim seek
the phronema of Crìost?
I know what I think
when I hear what I say;
I write what I say
to see how I think.
No vain monologue is this
but a dialogue with Crìost
who reframes what I say
and redeems inner sight.

Waymark 2

Intimacy

Letter to Anam-charaid

Dear Anam-charaid,
the door knocker
to your innerscape
protects the privacy of your soul.
Solas Chrìost
desires communion;
knocks, calls your name,
gains attention.
His unconsuming fire
warms your heart.
Flames engulf
your innerspace.

The Call

Ìosa Crìost, You call me to be with You.
Joyfully I come, for You I love.

I open my eyes to seek You,
close them to rest in You.

I abandon time, stay with You,
and breathe the fragrance of Your breath.

Lectio Divina

So the Lord called Adam
and said to him,
"Adam where are you?"

—Genesis 3:9 (SAAS)

Reflection

What dialogue
does the One-Who-Is-Three
seek with me?

Of relatedness:
what was, what is, and what is to come—
desire and expectation;
frustration and disappointment;
rigidity, chaos, and in between;
beginnings and endings;
disorientation and reorientation;
absence and presence;
barrenness and fecundity;
desolation, travail, and beatific life.

All in silent communion
with the Spirit of grace.

And my response,
what shall it be?
Complaints of a hard heart—
perversity, futility, and jeopardy?
Or ecstatic intimacy
to pursue the One-Who-Is-Three
with all my heart, mind,
soul, and strength?

PRAYER

Crìost, let me not mimic
our coming together this day.
Let me not settle for
a lover's desire, over-anxious in waiting,
wedged between promise and fulfilment,
that lets presumption's sway substitute
some concrete ritual in its place.

You come, knock at Your lover's door,
and there hear presumption's din,
the door closed to Your face.
Disappointed, You turn away,
shedding tears of grief.

O Ìosa Crìost! Let this never be again.

Contemplative Cue

Resurrect in joyful silence my waiting;
keep my door wide open to Your embrace,
to feel Your breath upon my face.

The Challenge of Trasna

Antipodean Courtship
(a fable)

Unimpeded ocean flows,
tempestuous winds, water, ice
encircle the realm of Southern isles,
volcanoes who defy ocean's writhe.

Here, two albatross wander,
feed, breed, dance together.
Courtship's unshattered dance binds
together till death, lovers forever.

But comes a day, a notorious act shatters;
a longline maelstrom snares her plumes;
his soul seared, her life broken—
an empty vestment beneath the waves.

The sun's fingers massage his back,
warm his skull, sinewed flesh, and breath.
His soul's confined by grief's spell
where dark spaces close light's door.

On the edge between external vestment
and internal truth, there is only grief—
a piercing blade, a desolate moment,
where dignity of his seared soul dissolves.

Desolation drives his soul to flee,
life's love stolen by human ways.
On huge broad wings he glides,
wanders wayward o'er Antipodes.

Alone on the wind, undisturbed
above crashing elusive waves,
over horizon's edge, the albatross
turns to face what's in his mortal midst.

Dawn's rays enter, darkness' edge flees,
and his Creator nudges within.
Gently through desolation's storm,
a courtship dance with Christ is born.

JOURNAL ENTRY

He asks, "Do you love Me?"
From unplumbed depths,
love draws words,
till I reimagine what is real.
Vows of love I take, words shaped
not by shallow adoption.
He asks again, "Do you love Me?"
My inner secular mode
prefers an order of things,
till Solas Chrìost upends my ways,
forms an intimate order.
He asks once more,
"Do you love Me?"

Waymark 3

Essence

.

Letter to
Anam-charaid

Dear Anam-charaid,
The essence of Crìost
was, is, and is to come,
the Word who was with God,
who is what God is.
The mystery of Crìost
is unfathomable.
Yet prior to any act of your existence,
before any stimuli aroused your intellect
or tingled your sensibilities,
the magnitude of His Being
was, is, and is to come
approachable.

His presence known,
His Word creates;
His love restores;
His power resurrects;
the Spirit transforms.
O that you might spend your days
chewing on this!

The Call

Let the phronema of Ìosa Crìost be ours:
His Living Word breathed through the ages.

May An Gèadh Fiadhaich guide
intuitions of faith and praxis.

Love penetrates thoughtful reflection;
practical wisdom lived: our vocation.

Lectio Divina

Who overcomes the world?
Is it not the one who believes
that Jesus is the Son of God?
This is the one who came by water and blood:
Jesus Christ; not with water only,
but with water and blood.
It is the Spirit who testifies,
because the Spirit is the truth.
There are three who bear witness in heaven:
the Father, the Word, and the Holy Spirit;
and these three are one.
And there are three that testify on earth:
the Spirit, the water, and the blood;
and these three agree as one.

—1 John 5:5–7 (EOB)

Reflection

Outside Eden's gates,
angelic guards wait with fiery swords,
blocking our way to the Tree of Life.
Beyond, lies Anthropocene's wastelands.
Here amid the thinness of smart technology,
the logic of post-modern minds,
many lived-meanings of good thrive:
old, recent, new ones birthed,
though not all blessed by God.

As we cross over thresholds
into unfamiliar places and spaces,
we sometimes uphold meanings of "good"
that deny love for our neighbor
and ignore communion with Ìosa Crìost,
the One who is our way to the Tree of Life.

PRAYER

Blessed Creator, let me sense
the Holiness of Your High Priest,
and with a priest's eyes on Earth,
see Creation bathed in grace.

Living Word, let me hear
with a prophet's soul
Earth's condition discerned,
Your pathos made known.

Holy Spirit, steep my mind
in wisdom's travail,
faith and love lived,
steeped in hope.

Triune God, interweave these three—
priest, prophet, counselor—
in harmony in me.
Take me deeper in
to follow You
as One-and-Three.

Contemplative Cue

Seek first the Three-in-One,
the One-as-Three in Heaven.
Hear by grace and communion
joys and tremors of God's revelation.
By this creative voice our worlds stand,
dissolve, or are suspended.
Shall we listen before we act?

How shall we discern the essence
of the Living Word?
By faith seeking understanding?
Yet how shall we reach beyond
understanding's torn veil?
By the witness of Spirit, water, and blood,
the Three who agree on Earth as One.

The Challenge of Trasna

Korimako Isles

(a fable about a most beautiful songbird—Korimako)

Last night in my dream,
An Gèadh Fiadhaich took me
to Heaven's birdsong isles.
I found myself in another living world,
bathed in ancient sounds rich in meaning,
in this age so beautiful to hear.

Admitted by spoken tongue used there,
my ears and speech questioning,
answering, understanding—and stumbling,
I taste sweet words on my tongue,
once mere fractured sounds,
that stir my mind and touch my heart.

Now listening to story-worlds
in treasured Korimako's tongue
of lives breathing now and in the past,
Korimako's world welcomes me
with patient eyes, melodic tongues.
Seeing me stumble, they pick me up,

They say to me: "Go further on,
seek the highest kowhai tree.
The sweetest nectar is not yet won."

Journal Entry

The pure light of Crìost
builds a temple within,
an unseen space
where Spirit dwells.
I find poetic imagination
evokes best His fire in my bones—
not so with philosophies and -ologies.
I circle, a hawk over its prey.
I often miss, yet I persist,
till one day the hunt is won.

Waymark 4

Angle of Vision

Letter to
Anam-charaid

Dear Anam-charaid,
see with naked eyes
the magnificent Crux:
four plus one stars anchored
in the Southern sky
on which we secure our bearings by.
Yet what seems so complete
is the treasured pupil
of heaven's eye,
where thousands of stars
glorify Sorchar nan Ruel.

The Call

God who divides light from darkness
refracts our sight to reveal the Divine spectrum,
reorients our mind and soul to Christ's:
His love and pathos illumed in prayer.

Unimagined refractions reveal where
Spirit leads:
voyage here.

Lectio Divina

Oh, the depth of the riches
both of the wisdom and knowledge of God!
How unsearchable are His judgments
and His ways past finding out!
For who has known the mind of the Lord?
Or who has been His counsellor?
Or who has first given to the Lord so as to be paid back?
Indeed, from him, and through him,
and to him, are all things.
To him be the glory unto the ages! Amen.

—Romans 11:33–36 (EOB)

Reflection

Suspend my tongue
between movement and containment.
Let memory of the intended creation
be reworked by tenacious revelation.
The jelling of what is "to be"
refined, mastered with care,
till the Spirit whispers:
"It is good."

Prayer

I pray to the Creator of Glory
through Christ, the One who lights the stars,
illume my heart with pure light;
open my inmost soul to Christ's light.
My eyes receive gifts of Divine wisdom,
enlightened to see Christ's refracted vision.
Holy Spirit, bless these gifts.
Reorient my condition.

Contemplative Cue

Primal disintegration of settled ways,
called into being by Christ to reach another,
trusted treasured conventions,
secure comforts of tradition,
ancient defences of social norms:
these let go to Christ.
Amid the dissonance of prayer,
the peace of Christ descends.
Amid primal disintegrations,
be strengthened—
God's Realm ascends.

The Challenge of Trasna

Beautiful One

(a tale of the banded dotterel)

There you are, beautiful one.
You've revealed yourself at last.
I hear your *twips*,
though you're hidden amid shells and sand.

I waited; you chose to show yourself.
You moved, stopped, walked, and stopped:
It's just how you walk,
feeding along the way.

On this sand-whipped spit,
you breed, come storm, flood, and surge.
Adept, here you raise your young.
O how Ìosa Crìost shines through you!

Journaling

My pen pivots;
I ponder which angles to pursue:
Perversity prefers the status quo—
but just stale journeys there.
Futility despoils my pen,
belittles the discipline to pick it up.
Jeopardy bleeds my pen
to appease my conscience, shame,
or someone's will.
Yet there is a way other than my own,
where my pen ploughs fallow ground with ink.

I turn back to the trial of Job:
Though three friends flayed his words,
Job searched his soul and candidly spoke.
Each friend, their own angle bent:
They contested experience,
echoed custom,
entrenched presumption.
All of them
were bewildered
when God broke in.

Waymark 5

Rhythm

Letter to Anam-charaid

Dear Anam-charaid,
to voyage
is to abandon yourself
to each unknown wave,
to lean into the breast of Crìost,
till the bower spray of broken waves
drips off your brow,
and there you listen
to the beating wings
of An Gèadh Fiadhaich.

The Call

Where my self-expression ends: silence.
There I sense Your rhythm for this day.

Your touch shifts my poise and pace;
in solitude, I sense Your kairos.

Sketch, wrangle, struggle,
wright words for Christ,
yet You call to me:
"Be still. Let words arrive."

Lectio Divina

You, Lord, in the beginning,
laid the foundation of the earth.
The heavens are the works of your hands.
They will perish, but you continue.
They all will grow old as a garment.
As a mantle, you will roll them up,
and they will be changed;
but you are the same.
Your years will not fail.

—Hebrews 1:10–12 (EOB)

Reflection

Rhythms change,
whereas formulas become feverish routines,
faith disrupted by the reliance on an act.
Different seasons, places, and spaces
I enter, get to know, and leave.
If intimate relations be absent
with the One-in-Three,
lost are sensibilities
to guide each step
through what lies
unknown
ahead.

Prayer

Creator,
bless to me this day
Heaven's dance on Earth
with the One-in-Three.

May I move in Christ's cadence
through each vulnerable position,
trusting, yielding, following Your lead.

The Paraclete outpoured
to steady mind, heart, and soul;
adjust my poise to Heaven's move.

Bless to me this day, Holy Trinity.
Redeem my condition,
encircle my dance on Earth
in grace.

Contemplative Cue

In the secret privacy of mind and heart,
where I fear God who knows what's there,
my Creator inserts between
yesterday's fight with tomorrow's life.
There, with rhythmic grace,
God divides light from darkness,
for Spirit desires neither rigidity nor chaos.
Her delight for me is to dance with Her,
Christ's unfolding choreography
in my most secret place.

The Challenge of Trasna

Pheasant Ways

Consider the pheasant:
she moves quite independently
in beautiful ways.

Alive by her wits,
she oscillates between appreciation
and defence. No place for pretence.

A vulnerable life: harried,
exploited, often betrayed.
Yet the rhythm of life
is revived each day.

And I too, though harrowed,
am restored. Christ permeates
the rhythm of my soul.

Journal Entry

Some things I write in retrospect,
like an enigmatic storm
that smashed rhythm's grip.
A moment to debrief
with An Gèadh Fiadhaich and me.
Yet there are things I'm not ready to write,
though I might say why or hesitate,
but not. As lines resolve, I pray:
"An Geadh Fiadhaich, intervene."
When I don't dig beneath rocks and clay,
infertile lines thwart my page.
All too often I'm prodded, stirred,
till Divine dissonance evokes fertile words.
This, I confess, takes days.

Waymark 6

Voice

Letter to Anam-charaid

Dear Anam-charaid,
Blessed is the voice
who knows how to speak
into our condition,
whose river of words
sparkles in Solas Chrìost,
whose silent ways
shine unspoken grace.

The Call

In human thickness of numb chat,
unbidden poetic voice breaks in.

People are provoked;
others hear hope—
resonances of difference.

Speak, poet, not as a dead fallen leaf.
Let your sap rise.
Bear truth's fruit.

Lectio Divina

O Lord, you who made the heaven,
the earth, the sea, and all that is in them;
who by the mouth of your servant, David, said,
"Why do the nations rage,
and the peoples plot a vain thing?
The kings of the earth take a stand,
and the rulers take council together,
against the Lord, and against his Christ.
And now, Lord, consider their threats
and grant your bond servants
to speak your word with all boldness."

—Acts 4:24–26, 29 (EOB)

Reflection

In the glens of a poet's wilderness,
where deep rivers are hard to cross,
there is one broken bridge
between wisdom's mind and soul's pulse,
guarded by hegemonic beings,
who rein in what may be said
on watch to decry communion
of the deepest movements
between Heaven and Earth.
They beguile the poet's tongue,
to be instead a mouth of a trout.
Yet Christ binds the evil one:
I shall cross that bridge
and follow where the Spirit leads.

And I appeal to Christ's reign
over every breath,
to touch mind and soul
with words I am to speak;
let no words be lost.
Christ, give heart to my tongue
with pathos and grace.
Anoint it with the overflowing oil
of Heaven on Earth.

PRAYER

Ìosa Crìost,
open up the way,
enfold my senses,
enlighten them to see.

Ìosa Crìost,
create from these a voice
to breathe into our condition,
into the breath of this age.

Lightener of the Stars,
empower imagination's work of truth,
spark a light within each soul,
and from there each mind renew.

Contemplative Cue

Is creation to be undone,
the sixth day cancelled?
The poet's light dimmed,
over-shadowed by futility?
Words formed to wander the Earth,
stillborn from procrastination,
banished till resurrected
from doubt's grave.

The Challenge of Trasna

Whose Spring Sings?
(a fable)

The messenger of spring,
flash-plumed pīpīwharauroa—
cryptic stripes, bronze on cream;
wings moss green—
arrives from migratory shores.
Her slurred upward whistle
beguiles riroriro's nesting place.

Riroriro, tiny tree-dwellers—
he heard, she rarely seen—
celebrate life in exuberant song,
harbingers of spring's hope, summer's reign;
beloved warbles soothe the land.

Riroriro checks the prevailing wind,
gathers feathers, hair, traces of wool.
Fibers blend and bend; a nest they weave,
a hanging dome from chosen tree,
hidden from vermin and summer wind,
a clutch of speckled eggs she lays.

Pīpīwharauroa knows riroriro's ways,
plunders riroriro's unguarded blessed nest.
Pīpīwharauroa raids, rules the nest,
kills the clutch—speckled eggs,
brood tossed outside—
brazenly lays counterfeit eggs,
and flees.

Not aware of counterfeit eggs,
a generation of song gone,
grief waylaid, riroriro fosters
imposters.
Nurtured counterfeits fly away;
their song mocks the empty nest.

As I heard this ancient tale,
a stranger turned, spoke to me:
"Whose song do you foster?
Whose song shall you praise?
Whose spring sings?
Whose song pervades?"

Journal Entry

O pen, in this hour;
exit, voice and loyalty.
How will you foray with these?
Shall passion's ink be lust for praise,
domination, and glory?
What living words—
gestated, birthed, and blessed—
shall shine Christ's Light
upon Anthropocene's wrath
against the life of the world?
Replace Anthropocene's ink
with the phronema of Christ.
Pen away with restorative grace.

Waymark 7

Reach

Letter to
Anam-charaid

Dear Anam-charaid,
Solas Chrìost
is a treasure to share, not hide.
The thisness of one soul
is not the same for another,
and so you are perplexed.
You wrestle in prayer
on how to reach
the thisness of another.
So abandoned be
ideology's presumption,
fear's censure. Speculation
too must flee. To reach another,
a mysterious voyage dawns
with An Gèadh Fiadhaich.

The Call

Your soul a poetic island
adrift on Anthropocene seas.

Come travail in prayerful whispers,
till your soul flies with An Gèadh Fiadhaich.

Travail till the poetry of your soul
dances before Sorchar nan Ruel.

Lectio Divina

However, we have this treasure
in vessels of clay,
so that the amazing power
may be from God and not from ourselves.
We are pressed on every side,
yet we are not crushed!
We are perplexed,
but not to the point of despair.
We are persecuted, yet not forsaken;
struck down, yet not destroyed.

—2 Corinthians 4:7–9 (EOB)

Reflection

Poetic words bear witness to life:
ecstatic joy or abyss of despair,
wonder or wreckage of creation,
or something in between.

An experience lived, revealed, imagined,
or some blend of these;
human sensations of relations, thought,
with Divine revelation interweaved.

Poetic witness of life,
words of power in exile
subtly waiting to be
situated, valued, and heard.

The after-words,
what follows on,
await to be written
by An Gèadh Fiadhaich.

PRAYER

Beloved Creator of Heaven and Earth,
what poetry rides on my breath?
A mere sonic vapor
that appears for a time
to vanish away?
And yet You
let it form on Earth,
and call it to roam on Heaven's breath.
By Christ's light, guide its unknown path
to touch a soul's most secret space.

Contemplative Cue

Let vulnerability be unleashed,
yet I be shielded by Christ.
Let no fear unnerve my heart,
nor rejection weary my soul.
Immerse this voyage of words
in Sabbath's strength.

The Challenge of Trasna

Bewildered
(a fable)

An elegant white hunter scythes waters
with black lips and red-ruby eyes.
Four little black shags watch
from sand wedged broken sticks
where river meets tide.

"Kōtuku-ngutupapa,
that's how we named her."
The elder spoke, then regaled her tale:
Out of elusive beginnings,
as dawn's mist arose, she just appeared.

Elegant Kōtuku-ngutupapa
over wild Southern oceans flew,
sought the Lightener of dawn's stars.
Head forward, legs trailing, plumes braced,
her restless desires sought gratification.

Empty horizons beckoned;
soul-weary, she fought futility's guile, till
Sorchar nan Reul, Jesus Christ,
Lightener of the Stars came beside.
His words redeemed discouraged eyes.

Spirit restored her heart,
plumbed the depths of her soul,
wrestled futility's contempt.
"Elegant Kōtuku-ngutupapa,
don't put a time-bind on God."

Lightener of the Stars warmed her heart,
spoke: "Who makes a wasteland?"
Said she: "Creatures deaf to Your call."
Christ asked: "Who makes a wilderness?"
"Those who seek You, follow Your call."

Lightener of the Stars stirred her heart.
"Look down, see where river meets tide.
Go amid this wasteland, Hymn to God
of wilderness, speak from your center.
Let them speak from theirs."

The Elder turned to the little black shags:
"Her flight disrupted, bewildered,
kōtuku-ngutupapa appeared,
hymned to Lightener of the Stars
The tide turned.
A wilderness is birthed here."

Journal Entry

What desires tear love apart,
hinders love's work for another?
Shall settled thresholds stay entrenched?
Availability postponed,
vulnerability censored,
generosity in peril—
or shall restorative grace encroach,
offer an open hand?

Waymark 8

Waypoints

Letter to Anam-charaid

Dear Anam-charaid,
are you bewildered,
beset with catastrophic anxiety,
disoriented thoughts?
Do you dismember all joy?
Let it disrupt your peace in Crìost?
O, how can you voyage
down unknown paths till
your eyes rest on Crìost,
not the shattered
rudder of your boat?

The Call

There are points along journey's way,
unknown times when voyages change.

We face powers of earth, sea, sky;
we confront intruding darkness.

Follow the One who overcomes
to be with those without an ark.

Lectio Divina

Also the Spirit helps our weaknesses,
because we do not know how to pray as we should.
But the Spirit himself makes intercession for us
with groanings which cannot be uttered.
He who searches the hearts
knows the way of thinking of the Spirit,
because the prayers that the Spirit makes for the saints
are always in accordance with God.

—Romans 8:26–27 (EOB)

Reflection

Expectations of security,
orientation, and certainties,
all overturned by leviathan storms.
Bewildered by disorientation,
we grapple for reorientation.
God's grace alone sustains us,
we modern Ninevehs.

Each storm we face a choice—
the way of Jonah: to flee,
our smouldering anger
confounding desire—
or the way of Paul:
to voyage on in Crìost,
all in all, here and there,
come what may.

Prayer

Almighty God, my Rescuer,
let Heaven's breath on Earth
inspire tongue, chest, and limbs;
encircle minds, hearts, and souls.
Keep my rudder from wayward paths;
protect my voyage from evil's guile,
yet may I be discerning and bold in Crìost,
who brings light to things hidden.
Bless my weave of words and deeds
in this disorientated world,
pointing eyes to the Tree of Life.

Contemplative Cue

Monstrous storms rage,
toss me into strange times.
Bewildered! I look around;
my limbs fall apart;
my chest melts like wax.
My tongue calls me to succumb:
to flee to safer parts, be among friends.
Yet some deeper stirring
speaks within my blood:
"Stay awhile, explore these times.
In faith look to the promises of God.
Journey amid understanding's torn veil.
Go where the inexplicable
and undefinable reveal
the wonderment of God."

The Challenge of Trasna

Deòir Dhè
(Tears of God)

Hear a story:

Rough storm breaks.
Sitting on dark ocean
amid surging waters,
a storm-petrel cries,
now with broken wing
from devouring fears, fashionable doubts,
powerful passions, wayward belief.

An Gèadh Fiadhaich
soars, searching, seeking.
Tender tears fall. She calls:
"Ìosa Crìost mends your wing,
renews mind, soul, and heart.
Come fly with me through every storm."
What song now will the petrel sing?

Journal Entry

When hope splinters, fear's malice
wedges shards, till ink erupts.
It bleeds, probes, rages, till the feed runs dry.
Another day, I refill my pen
ink surges: cathartic scribbles
lament a prayer for a way ahead.
Seasons pass. I turn the page.
Solas Chrìost shines,
and lines of grace find their place.
My pen nib now digs for wisdom's voice,
sieves words till ink
stains dire reality
with love's hope.

reach waypoints voyage intimacy essence
voice rhythm angle of vision

PART II

RUMINATIONS
ON PRAXIS

*Come, Living Word, weave Your design
into the fibers of my flesh.*

On Sightings

Each day, Solas Chrìost sighted.
Each night, Sorchar nan Ruel.
Each day, each night,
An Gèadh Fiadhaich calls the way.
A call heard,
fed by the Word;
norms provoked,
reflections evoked,
prayers travailed,
crossings faced:
journal updated.
And why? O what joy
to walk in the Light!

Letter to
Anam-charaid

To my anam-charaid,
the letter signed,
my name conveyed.
As ink dries,
may you become aware:
An Gèadh Fiadhaich
knows the thisness of each name.
Every unpredictable cause
and founding
coalesce in each breath of clay.
In each present moment,
we may have similarities,
speak of generalities,
yet no thisness is the same.

Under Solas Chrìost,
the hourglass turns.
Letters tell of thisness transformed,
God's grace and peace conveyed
by ink that signs our names.

The Call

To sense
the gentle fall
of virgin rain
on roaring surf
is to discern
the signature call
of An Gèadh Fiadhaich.
I call Ìsoa Crìost
who grants me the gift
to sense this fall
of virgin rain.

Lectio Divina

In silence
Your numinous beauty
anoints the words I recite.
My worship abounds with joy.
Sometimes I recite text
and wonder why.
Often I'm listening,
neither reading nor reciting,
only silent communion with Crìost.
Though wayward,
still I consume
the living Word.
I chew upon it,
and there Your grace
awakens me.

Your presence
consumes my absence.
My worship abounds
with joy.

Reflection

Celtic voyagers
are blessed with a gift,
a way of reflecting
they carry inside.
A poetic map
quite incomplete:
a progressive mosaic
of sensibilities and thoughts,
seasons and people,
spaces and places,
darkness and light,
all melded into one.

It's not so much
a geography alone,
nor a history alone,
nor an ethnography alone,
but more a transference of images
upon tectonic isles and wild seas.
A thin place:
a poetic innerscape
interweaving "was" with "is,"
with seasons and tides
and "is to come,"
revealed by Solas Chrìost.

`

Prayer

Usually I close
my eyes to pray,
not so much
to shut out the world
but to see the cross
of the crucified,
resurrected,
ascended Crìost,
whose Spirit
poured out
gives breath
to Heaven on Earth.
Now I pray
for the life of the world
in power and grace
with "Amen! Amen!"
pounding in my heart.

Contemplative Cue

At foredawn,
amid Antarctica's winter,
a momentary breath
rouses my mind
from timeless travels
to find itself iced
by seasoned lines,
disfigured by imposition
born of a fool's blood and self-will.
Yet there is a juncture
when dawn's melodies interrupt
discords of Antarctica's night.
Solas Chrìost melts my words;
my phronema renews
to keep its tryst with spring.

The Challenge of Trasna

The crossing over
the mountains of my mind,
the valleys of my heart,
the oceans of my soul,
An Gèadh Fiadhaich
evermore my guide.
Each crossing differs
from what's gone before.
Each one seems scalable
only in a dream.
Yet An Gèadh Fiadhaich
defrosts my blood, calls:
"Have you not come so far
for the purpose of this hour?"

Journal Entry

Sounds of ink on paper
are more than a memory;
they are alive, conversation
with An Geadh Fiadhaich
who traverses my innerscape,
creating language
by which I name
and explore spaces
that catch my eye,
that no other
but my Creator
has seen before.

Yet how much do I confess
or leave unsaid
with ink?
So much more is
silently inked
upon my soul.

PART III

SÙIL AN LATHA
(Eye of the Day)

As the Eye of the Day beams down

from foredawn to moonlight,

while a pilgrim reflects . . .

Sùil an Latha

(in the foredawn)

Crìost
I pray for the eye of an eagle
to soar, gazing upon purity:
the blazing white fire of Your eyes.
Yet under the Eye of the Day,
four ruses afflict my sight.
Each comes without asking
to form specks in my eyes.

I watch the Eye of the Day
from its rising till it sets.
At foredawn, I welcome
the rising sun as darkness flees.

At its zenith, heaven's light
dazzles my eyes.
When the sun dips over horizon's edge,
again I squint my eyes.
One last look as night arrives,
under the moon's reflective light.

Crìost,
at foredawn,
keep Antarctica's winds at bay.
Shield me from the coldness of heart,
the deathly chill that comes,
infuses mind and heart.
To thwart mercy's tongue,
Your restorative grace
wakes me, warms me
with the risen Son.

Crìost,
by the light of midday,
Earth's heat shimmers Your light.
In a hazy malaise,
my intellect, a gift received,
deceives itself,
crowns itself master,
not emissary of Crìost.
Irrupt into this haze;
lift my eyes to worship the Son.

Crìost,
in the light of gloaming
keep dragon-smoke at bay:
invasive clutter of day and night
enshrouds my sight,
overwhelms my sensibility,
disturbs our communion,
thwarts wisdom's discernment.

Crìost, come disperse the smoke.
Let truth triumph; deepen my sight.

Crìost,
by the moon's reflective light,
I have been consumed
by hedgehog moments.
For I have become on edge,
prickly, in some attempt
or pretence
to defend my dignity.
Instead, let love's wisdom
engage thought, heart, and deed.

Creator, Christ, and Spirit,
let my eyes be transformed
as I gaze with joy
with the eye of an eagle
into the eyes of Christ,
He who is brighter than the sun.
And I pray with the saints::
"Let it be."

Birth's Cry

(in the foredawn)

He thought his life's work done. And yet
an unhoped for voyage awaits
across the desert of mind and soul,
a confrontation to cast underfoot
the demon of nothingness
who contests God's Creation,
who numbs souls and minds,
beguiles them into nonbeing
to be welter and waste. Perturbed,
he wrestles, calling:

"Is this voyage to be my last,
before my birth? One last voyage
to put down this creeping nothingness,
this demon's shadow that stalks the faithful,
destroys hopes of animated breath,
intimidates hope's promise
in the voyage through death."

"Is this to be a prolonged birth," he asks,
"held in Earth's womb that my animated breath
be used once more? O, I have lived long!
No earthly desires remain;
my numbered days seem no more.
O, like Saint Paul, I yearn to leave,
made fully human—the glory of Christ,
resurrected in the image of God!"

"And why this delay?" he cries.
"I so desire to be born from Earth's womb
into the fullness of resurrected life.

When shall Earth's waters be broken?
Let the labour pains begin,
my birth into Christ's glory."

Yet he turns to face the One whose death
defeats death, resurrects life,
to be made fully human by grace
in the image of God, the glory of Christ.
So he calls upon the One
who creates light.
He calls upon the Living Word,
who out of nothing creates life.
He calls upon the Heavenly Host,
as did the saints through the ages,
to encircle each step of the way.

He acknowledges:
"My breath soon must cease.
Aged and weary, my work is done,
or so I thought.

This is no lament,
no complaint like Job,
no question of 'to be or not to be?'"

But might he pray,
"Deliver me from this trial"
or simply say, "Let it be"?
For the love of the stranger, O let it be!
For the love of neighbor,
for the love of God.

"Unleash once more Your mighty power," he cries.
"Vivify my weary flesh, my tired breath.
And I too shall face, as did the saints,
the demon of nothingness
that infests mind and soul,
who by stealth drains the heart."

"I shall rest my head,
as did the Desert Fathers,
upon the breast of Christ,
my weak flesh enlivened by the Living Word,
my breath nourished by the Spirit.
And I shall drink from the chalice,
eat shared bread."

"If 'let it be,'
my vessel awaits:
all the wisdom and power of Christ
a fire rekindled in the marrow of old bones.
Let my martyrdom on Earth be
in the fullness of time,
bearing fruit with joy."

Forever Held

(under midday sun)

I bend my knees to You, my God.
Let not my barrenness shape my soul.
Am I reaching, striving for a dream,
to pluck fruit out of reach, in vain?

Birth a seed in my spirit's womb
that I behold its fruit with joy.
Or am I wrangling a tree of dreams
that will not bend nor yield to me?

Shame, at its zenith a piercing sun,
desiccates all strength to dream.
Thousands of sunrises of yearning
thousands of sunsets of weeping,
as hope's subsidence turns to mourning,
desire's loss purchased with pain.
But let Your presence sustain my flesh,
a bond unseen forever held.

O, I tread on exhausted dreams,
secret dreams that shape my face.
Might one ignite swift joy of heart,
kindle rejoicing of womb and breath?

Mortal Bones

(under midday sun)

Our bones enfleshed arose by birth;
each mortal breath seeks fulfilment:
the cusp of present moments.
Is not this the fullness of time!

We can watch sand fall
grain by grain in the hour glass.
But without our minds' creation,
times past and future cannot exist.

And what threads of memories remain when
mortal bones fall beneath the weight of sand?

Let our temporality meet
eternity in the fullness of time.

The uncreated Son of God
created, a child from Mary's womb.

Again let our temporality meet
eternity, the fullness of time.

The Son of God on the cross,
the moment of our transformation.

The eternal power of God moving
in and through us in earthly time.

Shadows Go

(in the gloaming)

At the end of the day,
on a hill close to the edge,
they come but go no farther.
In human strength, they trust;
handle their pain, mirth, and love;
surf their emotions,
dance to their thoughts,
fight their fears alone,
and let their tears overflow.
When love
does not grow, they hide inside
where shadows grow.

So many shadows
that make them bend.
O! let one eternal light
be found inside come Lent.
And on Paschal's Day,
O come! Let them rise
with the morning sun
and rejoice with all
who let their shadows go.

Time of Gifts

(in the gloaming)

The voyager wept,
for this was him:
pieces of broken shell
tossed upon a migrant's shore.
Here indigenous he can never be.

He is tangata tiriti,
who stands upon broken shells,
remnants of empire's permafrost.
Shielded from ancestral traumas
by assimilation's work.

Not all stories are subsumed;
remnant strands remain,
fragments handed down
of dùthchas nan Gaidheal,
memories of indigenous lands.

To him, dùthchas nan Gaidheal
a hidden treasure, a gift almost lost.
Indigenous tongue, its poetic beauty spurned.
Sounds, colors, and smells,
indigenous ways of Gael and Pict,
rely on others memories, hand-me-downs.
Yet ancient winds still stir ancestral bones,
whose voices speak from unknown graves
of ways Crìost moved amid woven clans.

And deep in his blood, he desires
He who was, is ,and is to come,
the One who rejoices
in nan Gaidheal Christian past,
the One who knows the words
his ancestors heard as Calum Cille spoke
and how Solas Chrìost encircled
their splintered lands from sea to sky

He who was, is, and is to come
again gathers broken shells,
washes each with tears,
melds them like paua,
till plaid colours form
and flicker new dawn's light.
Now Crìost moulds them,
fashions a high Celtic cross.

East and west faces He makes,
reveals the finished work of Crìost.
He places the cross, raises it high
between Heaven and Earth,
seen from the Sun's rising-place
to the setting of foredawn's stars.
This sign of Life since the first of times
was, is, and is to come
a gift from Crìost.

Thin Places

(by moonlight)

What is ninety-five years to an ice flow?
Creation's sound of time itself:
raging clouds full of thunder
dump snow upon the high places.
It falls and slides into circques below,
shatters rock, grinds mountains down,
gravitates toward ocean waves,
and there it calves, slowly melts away.
This sight consumes all breath
in awe and wonder all I do
is worship my Creator.

But when does a wild place
become a thin place,
must they reside in seeds of wonder?
Are they special places
where communion is easy
between Heaven and Earth
where life slows down
to a glacial pace
and wayward ways calve from my flesh?

And is a sacred place a thin place
where ancient traditions bequeath
treasured assurance—love's wisdom,
where mercy meets the truth of Christ,
beatitudes point to the way of life,
and justice is kissed by peace?

What is a thin place?
A listening place
where time is desynchronized,
and eternity glimpsed,
a kaleidoscope of Heaven on Earth,
seeing, not judging,
but like Saint John, seeing Crìost move
both in Heaven and on Earth.

Such a place—not made by hands of clay
but a gift of Crìost by the way of the cross—
makes joy well up at unexpected times
amid the rhythm of the day.
Come, Ìosa Crìost, come!
That I may be alert to the thin places,
wild, sacred, and within.

Odyssey To Be

(by moonlight)

Crìost-in-me is awe of Creation.
Crìost-in-me is a mountain to climb.
Crìost-in-me is a voyage of grace.
Crìost-in-me gives me grit to journey.
Crìost-in-me is the power of the Spirit.
Crìost-in-me is my joy of communion.
Crìost-in-me is the bread of life.
Crìost-in-me is peace amid strife.
Crìost-in-me is love of my neighbor.
Crìost-in-me is helping the stranger.
Crìost-in-me is beauty from ashes.
Crìost-in-me is my odyssey to BE,
for without Him,
I could never BE.

About the Author

Poet Craig A. Roberts, tangata-tiriti, lives between the mountains and the sea on Kapiti Coast, Aotearoa New Zealand, near a mountain called Kapakapanui. From the mountain's slopes and valleys flow the waters of the Waikanae River. Craig's father's forbears left their mountains and valleys of Scotland's central Highlands, and his mother left the fields of Northumbria. Over the generations, the journeys of Craig's forebears brought them to these antipodean isles.

Craig worked alongside leaders on the frontiers of change amid turbulent worlds. An applied social scientist, he holds a PhD in follower-centered leadership. Nowadays, he writes through a Celtic lens on the restorative grace of Solas Chrìost transforming yesterday's fight with tomorrow's life.

Waymarks is an uncompleted map of his voyage so far to renew his phronema with the phronema of Ìosa Crìost. To find out more about him, go to:

https://craigrobertsauthor.com

Also by Craig Roberts:

Slow Wisdom: A Forgotten Virtue

This Cave Beside Me
(a poetic tale exploring life after death)

Vocation as Resistance:
God Moving Through, In, Before, & Beyond us

Serenity: Celtic Poetry to Bring Us Closer to God

Tree of Life
Celtic Prayers to the Universal Christ

*Christ is the visible image of the invisible God. He existed before
anything was created and is supreme over all creation,
for through him God created everything. . . .
He existed before anything else, and he holds all creation together.*
—Colossians 1:15–17

Like a vast, ever-growing Tree of Life, Christ—the expression
of Divine love—expands endlessly throughout the universe.
This is the perspective of ancient Celtic spirituality, and it is
this concept that Ray Simpson reveals in his poem-prayers.
Inspired by the traditional Celtic style of prayer, he gives words

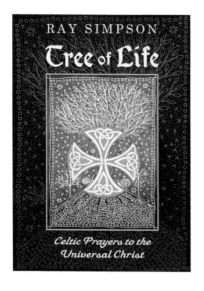

to our individual
relationships with
God. He speaks of the
wonder, beauty, and
love revealed through
the Universal Christ,
the Tree of Life that
includes all that is.
Each and everything
in creation is sacred,
for everything is a
word of God—and we
too are called to be
God's words to
our world.

Shalom!

Celtic Prayers for Wholeness and Healing

Although we often think the definition of shalom is "peace," the Hebrew word encompasses far wider meanings, including completeness, well-being, safety, prosperity, contentment, health, friendliness, and rest. Shalom implies the divinely ordained state of well-being, of justice, equity, and fulfilment, which God wants for each of us as individuals and for all of us as communities. It's a state of harmony, an interwoven connection that supports and nourishes both the parts and the whole.

We need shalom in our bodies, our minds, and our spirits—and we need it in our relationships and in our communities. In these prayers, Ray Simpson invites us to offer up all that is broken or unhealthy, so that we can experience the full meaning of shalom.

Celtic Prayers for
the Rhythm of Each Day

Every hour is holy,
every day is sacred

We sometimes think prayer belongs only in certain places on certain days. This book calls us to set prayer free from these constraints, allowing it to flow out through the hours of every workday, sanctifying the ordinary rhythm of our modern lives.

Ray Simpson gives us twenty original prayers, written in the Celtic tradition or patterned after ancient Celtic prayers, for each interval of the day. Like generations of earlier followers of Christ, we too can use prayer to bless the rhythm of our daily lives, infusing the hours with the awareness of the One who gives us Life. These small pauses throughout the day will make us ever more aware that the Kingdom of Heaven is a constant and present reality, hidden just beneath the veil of everyday life.

The Hidden Way

Celtic Prayers for the Spiritual Journey

*Join Ray Simpson in prayer as
you follow the hidden way to spiritual life.*

Ray Simpson has spent his life following the mystic's path that lies hidden in the midst of everyday life. This path is also the heart of Celtic Christianity: simply following in Christ's footsteps in the ordinariness of life. From this perspective, everything becomes an act of spiritual meaning—

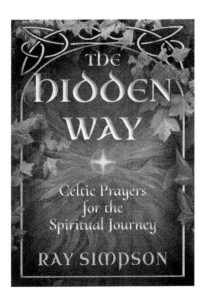

getting up in the morning and going to bed at night, going to work and playing with children, suffering pain and rejoicing in pleasure, working together in friendships and families and communities.

Paths of Justice

Celtic Prayers for a World of Equity, Unity, and Healing

Energize us with Your compassion, Giver of Life, to help the dispossessed, to listen to those without voices, and to reach out in friendship to all. Empower us with Your love; encourage us with Your Spirit; make us strong to bring Your justice to individuals, communities, nations, and the entire globe.

Our society often assumes that "justice" has to do with punishment. We think it means we make criminals pay for their crimes. The biblical meaning of the word "justice," however, means "to make right." This concept of justice has to do with healthy relationships

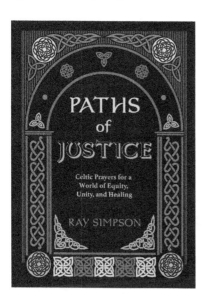

based on equity and kindness; it refers to a society based on life-giving relationships between God, human beings, and the natural world. This is the world Ray Simpson seeks to build, and he offers these prayers as openings into the Divine power that constantly seeks to heal and restore.

Celtic Christianity
Deep Roots for a Modern Faith

The world of the long-ago Celts appeals to many of us in the twenty-first century. Whether we are looking to find our cultural heritage or are seeking an alternative to worn and restrictive religious forms, the Earth-centered, woman-friendly, inclusive faith of the Christian Celts offers us a deep-rooted alternative approach to traditional Christianity. The Celts experienced "thin places," where they sensed the supernatural world; they honored their poets, singers, and artists; and they passionately followed the Christ of the Gospels. Theirs was a church without walls, which lived naturally and comfortably within the community. Ray Simpson has spent most of his life walking in the footsteps of the Christian Celts, and now he allows us to experience for ourselves their dynamic spirituality.

deep roots for a modern faith

RAY SIMPSON

AnamcharaBooks.com

Printed in Great Britain
by Amazon

44305649R00118